CONTENTS

Words in **bold** are explained in the glossary.

Insects

The bugs in this book are **insects**.

There are more insects in the world than any other creature. They live in many different **habitats**, from hot, dry deserts to underwater!

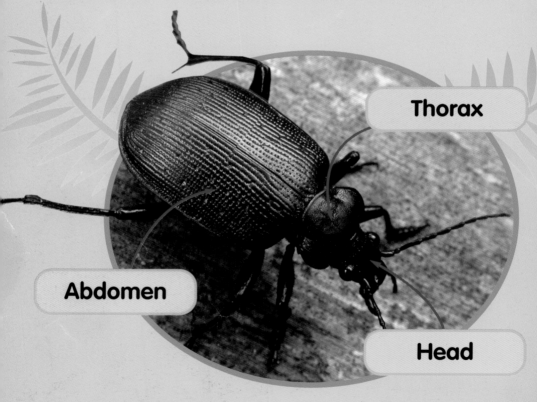

Thorax

Abdomen

Head

There are insects of many different shapes and sizes, but they all have a body made up of three parts.

Most insects have two antennae...

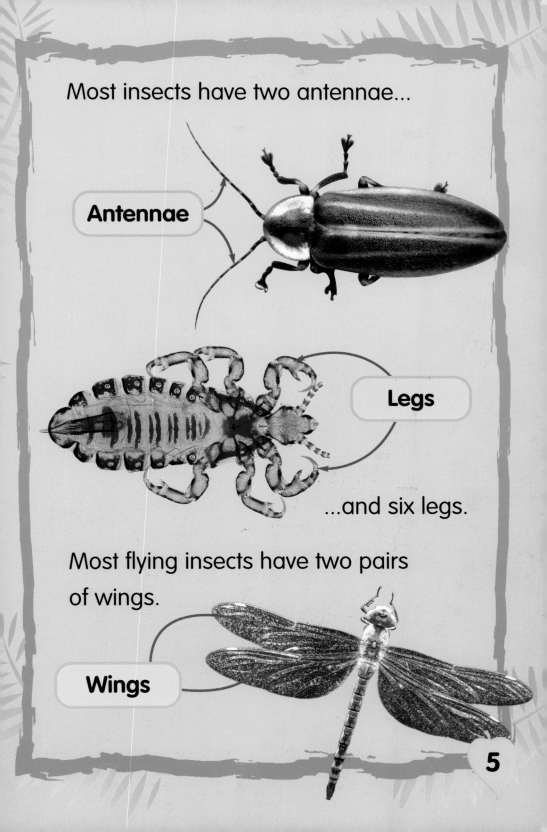

Antennae

Legs

...and six legs.

Most flying insects have two pairs
of wings.

Wings

Ladybirds

There are many different kinds of ladybirds. Most are red with black spots.

Head

Thorax

Abdomen

There are also yellow ladybirds with black spots and black ones with yellow spots!

They can all fly.

6

Their bright colours tell **predators**, such as birds, that they do not taste very nice.

Aphids

Ladybirds live in gardens and parks. They feed on small bugs called aphids.

Ants

Ants live almost everywhere in the world. They live in **colonies** with other ants.

Ants eat other insects. They also eat the **honeydew** made by aphids.

Head

Antennae

Thorax

8

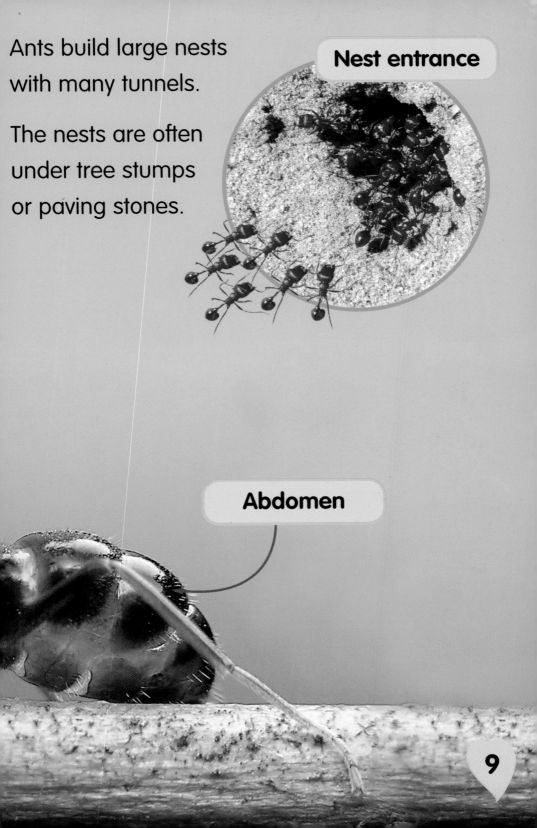

Ants build large nests with many tunnels.

The nests are often under tree stumps or paving stones.

Nest entrance

Abdomen

Dragonflies

The dragonfly is the fastest flying insect in the world.

Head

Wing

Thorax

Abdomen

10

There are more than 5,000 different kinds of dragonflies.

Dragonflies live near ponds, lakes, streams and rivers.

An adult dragonfly has a long body. It uses its long, thin wings to hover in the air and dart around. It can even fly backwards!

Dragonflies feed on flying insects. Sometimes they eat other dragonflies.

Butterflies

There are many different kinds of butterflies.

They have long antennae and their brightly coloured wings are covered with thousands of tiny **scales**.

Proboscis

Butterflies have a long tongue like a straw, called a proboscis. They use this proboscis to drink **nectar** from flowers.

Antennae

Some butterflies live for many years. Others live for about a week. Some only live for a day!

13

Head lice

Head lice are about the size of a pinhead.

They live on clean hair and feed on human blood.

They have little hooks on the end of their legs.

They hook their short legs around the hair.

Abdomen

14

Head lice do not have wings so they cannot fly.

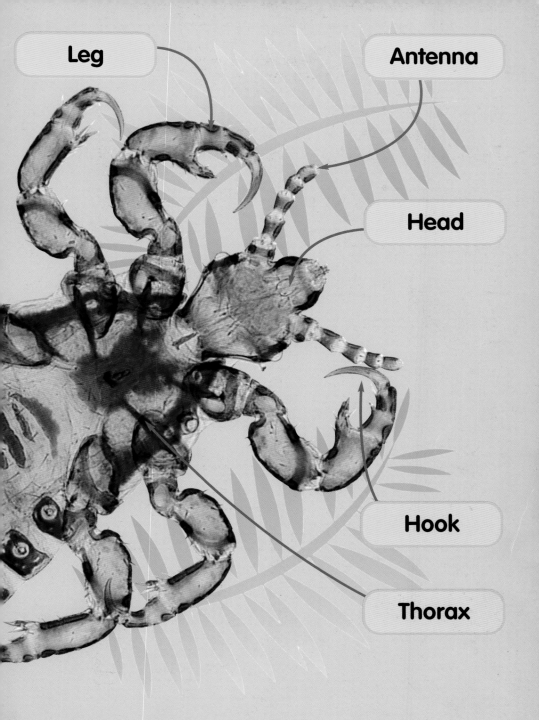

Leg

Antenna

Head

Hook

Thorax

They use their legs and hooks to crawl from head to head.

Aphids

Aphids are tiny insects that live on plants and trees.

They suck **sap** from the leaves and **shoots** of young plants. This damages the plant and makes it weak.

Aphids

Aphids are the main **prey** of ladybirds.

Aphids make honeydew which is eaten by ants.

Ant

17

Insect life cycles

All insects begin life as eggs laid by an **adult**.

They change as they get older.

Some insects change twice in their lives.
They change from an egg to a nymph, then
to an adult.

Dragonfly

Aphid

Head louse

Aphids, head lice and dragonflies
change like this.

Dragonfly life cycle

Eggs

Nymph

Adult

More life cycle changes

Some insects change three times in their lives.

They change from an egg to a larva, then to a pupa and finally to an adult.

They look very different each time they change.

Butterfly

Ladybird

Ant

Ants, ladybirds and butterflies change like this.

Caterpillar

A butterfly larva is called a caterpillar.

Ladybird life cycle

Eggs

Larva

Pupa

Adult

Glossary

adult
Fully grown up.

colonies
Large groups of animals living together.

habitats
The place that is just right for a particular animal or plant in the wild.

honeydew
A sweet liquid made by aphids.

insects
Small animals with bodies that have three parts.

nectar
A sweet liquid in flowers.

predators

Animals that hunt and eat other animals.

prey

An animal that is hunted by another animal for food.

sap

A liquid in plants and trees.

scales

Small, overlapping sections of skin.

shoots

Sections of new growth on plants.

Index

Copyright © **ticktock Entertainment Ltd 2008**
First published in Great Britain in 2008 by **ticktock Media Ltd.,**
Unit 2, Orchard Business Centre, North Farm Road, Tunbridge Wells, Kent TN2 3XF
ISBN 978 1 84696 769 6 pbk
Printed in China

We would like to thank: Penny Worms, Shirley Bickler, Suzanne Baker and the National Literacy Trust.

Picture credits (t=top, b=bottom, c=centre, l-left, r=right, OFC= outside front cover)
Science Photo Library: 7. Shutterstock: 8-9, 10, 16-17, 18-21. Superstock: 11, 17tr. ticktock photography: 4, 5, 6, 12-13.

Every effort has been made to trace the copyright holders, and we apologise in advance for any unintentional omissions. We would be pleased to insert the appropriate acknowledgements in any subsequent edition of this publication.